I Wish I Could Tell You:

Pearls of Wisdom from Grannie

by

Marcia H. Walker

Dorrance Publishing Co
585 Alpha Drive
Suite 103
Pittsburgh, PA 15238
Visit our website at *www.dorrancebookstore.com*

ISBN: 979-8-8872-9043-0
eISBN: 979-8-8872-9543-5

"Table of Contents"

<h1 style="text-align:center">*"Dedication"*</h1>

This is written for my granddaughter, Avery, who is my Pure Joy and Precious Jewel. You are my "PJ"! While I wrote this book for Avery, it may be of value to others. So, that you can relate to the references to PJ you are also my PJ as "Pursuers of Joy" or as a Partner on life's Journey, i.e., We all want more joy and in many ways most of us compare what we know with what we have done with what we believe etc. to what new information we come across. I hope that your journey through this book brings you more joy and understanding of your personal journey.

I am sharing pearls of wisdom that I hope you will take on your life's journey. These pearls will make sense at different times in your life. I understand that you have a mind of your own and at times may not want to hear or read what I am sharing. Just know that this is written in love and with the hope that you will have a good and wonderful life, but also a blessed life, filled with grace and favor. I also pray that you will be a person who will show grace and favor to others as well.

I wish that someone had told me many of these things so I wouldn't have had to learn some hard lessons on my own. I see now that in order for me to grow, I had to learn and survive them. Just like the caterpillar has to struggle to break from the cocoon to become a beautiful butterfly, so there will be times that you too will struggle. My intent is to share some things that just might help the struggles and experiences in life make some sense. If I had the opportunity, I wish I could tell you all of these things, because I love you so much and I am cheering you on to have a good life and a wonderful journey of discovery!

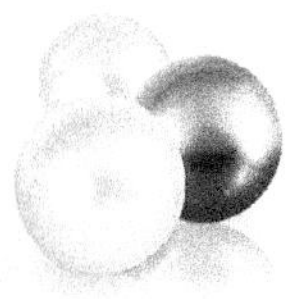

Pearl #1:
I wish I could tell you about the consequences and benefits of your choices.

I wish I could tell you that we all need a strong foundation to stand on throughout life. Much of that foundation is made up of our belief system, your values and principles on which you will operate. What you believe and your decisions about what is right or wrong comes from your foundation and what kind of person you aspire to be.

All through life, every day, everyone makes decisions and choices based on their foundational thinking/feelings of what they understand to be right/wrong, good/bad, okay/not okay or in their best interest or not in their best interest, and you too will have to make those decisions. For example, is it okay to steal, lie, not keep commitments, be respectful or not be respectful, care about others or only be concern with ourselves? PJ, by what standards will you live and make your choices every day?

How do you develop behaviors and ways of thinking that defines the kind of person you want to be? In many cases the family we grow up in establishes some of our foundation. What is taught and what examples do you see at home? What examples do you observe? What is expected at school? How should you behave on the playground, grocery store or anywhere in public, at home at work? How do you treat your toys/belongings, or the toys/belongings of others? Is it okay to kick/hit others when you are angry, or things don't go your way?

Parents gives rules of behavior that is acceptable within their family. Most parents want their children to have a level of freedom to express themselves and their emotions. As you grow, you will experience a variety of experiences that will cause you to react in a variety of ways. You will explore situations that will vary from making you happy, sad, unhappy, confused, disappointed and angry. You will have a range of emotions. You will need to make choices about how you will react in each of the situations that you will experience. Keep in mind, everyone, every day, have a variety of circumstances that they have to decide about what they think and what they will do. All through life, even as an adult, you will have to decide every day how you will react or respond to the circumstances you will encounter.

I wish I could tell you that there will come a time when you must decide your personal standards, values, and morals for yourself. Who do you want to be, what kind of person are you and how do you choose to behave? I wish I could tell you that while your family might have some influence, it is your life that you are accountable for, and YOU have to be willing to accept and own the consequences or benefits of the choices you make.

I wish I could tell you that while there will always be ups and downs throughout life, Life really isn't that complicated. I hope the few "pearls" I am sharing will give you a perspective to consider and an understanding to make some sense of that that may not make sense at the time.

I wish I could tell you to
Embrace your negative emotions.
They are bubbling to the surface
in search of attention.
Be thoughtful to what the negativity is telling you
about what is going on inside of yourself
that is needing you to attend to it
as if it is not any different than any other
unexplainable pain, illness, or circumstance.
I wish I could tell you that the challenges in your
life happen for a reason to build your sense of self,
your character, your strength, and to define who
you are and who you ain't!
Don't shy away from your challenges, or adversity
they have an ultimate positive purpose!
Unplanned, unexpected and unwanted events and
people happen for a reason.
What have they come to teach you or help you to develop?

Pearl #2:
I wish I could tell you about the God I know.

Even as a little child I experience a concept called God. I believe that God is the creator of everything and everyone on earth. In this world, I have come to see God in all of nature, the complexities, and interdependence of animals and human beings.

Just imagine, what had to happen as you grew inside of your mom. Every part of you came from cells designed by God specifically for you. Imagine, all of the intricacies that had to happen during the nine months you were in your mother's womb to form every aspect of your body, mind, spirit, and soul. WOW, you are one of a kind! There is no one else exactly like you! You are special! You are unique!

I call you PJ, because I see you as a Precious Jewel and you are especially my Pure Joy! I thank God that I lived to hold you as a baby and to see you develop into a wonderful, talented, amazing, intelligent, and kind individual. I wish I could tell you how much I love you and how proud of you I am.

I wish I could tell you that you are a very special gift from God. Sometimes we think we know what we want, but God knows what we need. More importantly, each of us has a purpose for our existence. What I mean is that God created each of us to accomplish certain things that are unique to each person. What I do may be different than what you or your mom might do. It may even have some similarity but done differently based on the talents and abilities God gave each of us.

You are His child in whom He has put great things. While God is always present, you can't see Him, but somehow you know He exists. Because you can see Him in all of the various creations and marvel at them. Thinks about your own body. Your heart beats automatically and all of the functions in your body that operate without you doing anything. Eating properly and doing all you can to stay healthy is so important.

I pray that you are willing to understand that there is a God of this world, The 10 Commandments gives us guideposts for how we should behave. They really are not that difficult, first of all to seek God and always be respectful of Him. The other rules are to be honest, love others, be kind, don't take anything that does not belong to you, be respectful and honor your parents. I believe that Jesus died so that we can live our lives, feeling confident that God forgives our weaknesses and has more awaiting us beyond this life, called heaven.

He created it, the land, sky, waters, and all of the creatures - I wish I could tell you to be opened to receive God not as a fairy tale or irrational thinking, but as the wonderful,   glorious truth of our Lord, our Father, our Creator, God Almighty. I wish I could tell you and you would listen and be willing to seek after Him!

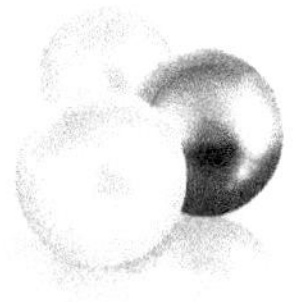

I wish I could tell you that people who have hurt you, often are people who are hurting. I wish I could tell you that you are stronger and able to rise above what they say or do. I wish I could tell you that that which was meant to hurt, really can build your character, your resolve, and your ability to be a better person than those who malign you.

I wish I could tell you not to carry the hurt, nor see it as a crutch to carry through your life's journey. I wish I could tell you, what happened yesterday, should not be expected in today, nor cripple you, nor be your excuse for who you do not become or do tomorrow. I wish I could tell you, "Rise - step on and over the hurts to Rise – above the pettiness of others."

I wish I could tell you that while you can't undo what has been said or done, but you can take those hurts and the pain as an overcomer and in spite of any devastation they may have caused … you be the victor, not a victim. PJ, I wish I could tell you that!

Pearl #4:
I wish I could tell you that there are better days ahead no matter the struggle.

Today is only a steppingstone to your future. I wish I could tell you that you have a choice to learn from whatever and whoever happened today. It is your choice whether you learn that sometimes things and people just happen. You are not being singled out. Stuff happens to everyone. I wish I could tell you it is more about how you chose to allow whatever negative things or people affect you. It is your choice whether you give an incident or an individual more importance in the overall scheme of things than they rate.

I wish I could tell you to choose to give situations, people, and yourself grace. Grace that all situations are teachable and character-building opportunities. Seize the opportunity to learn and to be kind and forgiving of situations, others and especially yourself. Adversity's intention is to test you. Who you are really and how the "real" you will show up in an adverse situation or with a rude, toxic individual? Will you be the positive light? Will you exchange toxicity with toxicity? Or will you tell yourself, I will not let this adverse situation turn me into a reaction that isn't the person I aspire to be. I wish I could tell you that how you "show up" in adversity is really who you are. Who are you really? And is that the person you really really want to be? Who do you want to be PJ?

I wish I could tell you that you want to be the better person. I wish I could tell you to not let anything, any situation or anybody affect you in any way different than who you aspire to be. I wish I could tell you to rise above negativity, but it is your choice.

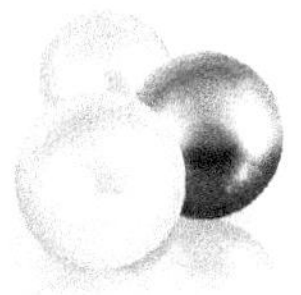

Pearl #5:
I wish I could tell you about the power of forgiveness.

I can tell you that sometimes what others do and say, really hurt down deep, whether that was their intention or not. When someone spills unkindness, rudeness, and even intentional meanness on us, we have a choice to respond in kind or…? I once heard a saying, "You can't throw dirt, without getting your own hands dirty."

I wish I could tell you that we are all part of the construction crew. Sometimes the crew is tearing down and other times the crew is building up. It is all about intent and impact. What are your intentions when you are tearing down or when you are building up? I am telling you to examine your intention, as well as your impact. Sometimes that which is well intentioned, is not invited. Develop the ability to forgive yourself and others, however, that does not mean that you are weak or allowing yourself to be a doormat. Let others know when they have crossed a boundary and your expectations for their behavior towards you in the future. If they don't honor your boundary, then you make a choice about whether and/or to what extent they will be in your life in the future.

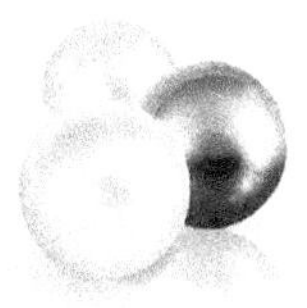

I want to tell you that you have a responsibility for how you show up. We all know people that we walk on tippy toes around when they show up. We are not quite sure what kind of mood they are going to be in or how approachable they might be. When that person shows up, they create an intensity that affects the environment and everyone in it, most often in a negative way. Don't be that person whose behavior and demeanor are so unpredictable people avoid you. I wish I could tell you always leave a situation and others better than before you showed up!

Pearl #7:
I wish I could tell you that
there are no failures.

I wish I could tell you that there are no failures, just lessons learned. I wish I could tell you that throughout life, you are building a reference library with every experience, person, and situation you encounter. That reference library is how you navigate through life by building on lessons learned, whether the lessons are the result of mistakes or victories. Learn from them. I wish I could tell you that when you don't, the lesson continue to repeat over and over until you do learn what life is trying to teach you.

I wish I could tell you that everyone is not going to love or like you, and PJ that is okay. I want to tell you that it is okay to be different, and to not fit in. God made you unique for the plans He has for you. Celebrate your uniqueness. Be happy when you find yourself alone. Being alone gives you time to reflect, pray and celebrate who you are. I wish I could tell you how special you are, and that you do not need the approval or acceptance of others who cannot or will not celebrate who you are.

I wish I could tell you that in life, there will be many different people who will hitch themselves to your wagon. I wish I could tell you that all will have good intentions, but that is not true. As you are navigating through your unique journey through life, there will be some that will try to distract you, there will be some whose negativity will affect your self-confidence, that is, if you let them. There will be people who will try to derail your direction, because they want you to go their way, choose wisely to go the way God is leading you.

There will be others who have no direction and will make fun of your direction. Direct them out or off your wagon. I wish I could tell you that everyone who smile your way are not intended to be with you for the long haul. Some people are only on your wagon for a season. I wish I could tell you that seasons are just a period of time. You have to have discernment to know when a season has changed and is over. I wish I could tell you to learn what you need to learn, do what you need to do and go when you need to go forward without anything or anyone whose season has ended on your journey.

I wish I could tell you that it is important and imperative that you love yourself. I don't mean in a conceited way or in an obnoxious or arrogant manner. Be a person on a mission to accomplish all that God has put inside of you. Trust that the Holy Spirit will speak to your heart and lead your soul to do what is right for you and to have the strength to say no to that, that is not right for you.

I will tell you that God loves you. I will tell you that even though life sometimes throw mud and obstacles in your path, trust God has your back and only wants good for you. There are tests of your faith, trust and belief in God, even in the hard times. There are so many blessings that come after, and even during the tests. I wish I could express how wonderful your blessings will be, but it is your journey PJ, and you will just have to see for yourself.

Pearl #9:
I wish I could tell you to let go of
deadness in your life.

Things, situations, and peoples' impacts die. I wish I could tell you how useless, toxic and a time waste it is to carry dead things, situations and what someone has done or said with you long after they need to be buried in the useless cemetery. I wish I could tell you how energy draining and time wasting it is to dwell on things, people and situations that have hurt you. I wish I could tell you not to waste your time and future on things, situations, and people you cannot change, or sometimes understand.

Whatever you lost, whatever happened or whatever was said, take from it that that makes sense to you and leave the rest in the past. Your future is waiting and needing your energy and focus to get to where God is leading you. I wish I could tell you that SOS means different things, depending on the situation. I wish I could tell you not to let people or situations that are **Stuck on Stupid** slow you down or misdirect you from **Sailing on Straight** ahead. My dear, I wish I could tell you to keep your sails full of positivity on your journey. Allow life's winds to compel you onward! **Learn - Grow - Go!**

Pearl 10:
I wish I could tell you
how important today is.

I wish I could tell you how important today is; in fact, this moment is all you have right now. The next moment just might not come, or it could change everything, savor this moment for all that it is giving you. Don't waste this moment over-thinking yesterday or worrying about tomorrow. Enjoy right now as fully as you can. I wish I could tell you how many people regret that they wasted time and opportunities to enjoy their families, their individuality, or their right now. They filled their time with the pursuit of things, situations and people who did not bring the joy they expected. Don't let your ego pursue what has poor returns on the investment of valuable time from your life. Don't waste your life, pondering regrets, if I coulda, woulda, shoulda all waste precious moments you will never get back.

Pearl #11:
I wish I could tell you that anger hurts.

I wish I could tell you that anger hurts you. A minute of anger takes away sixty seconds of joy from your life. How many seconds of joy can you afford to lose to a burst of anger? I wish I could tell you to examine your anger, before expressing it. Examine what are you angry about and then why are you angry about it? Is it about you, something in the past that is unresolved or the situation, person, or issue in front of you?

Anger affects you, your body, your mind, and your spirit in multiple ways. Anger creates energy surges, and when energy surges occur, chemicals such as adrenaline enter your bloodstream, your heart rate increases, your blood flow increases, and your muscles tense. Losing your temper affects your cardiac health. It can shorten your life when it is sustained. I wish I could tell you that anger increases your blood pressure and strains your heart health. I wish I could tell you to ask yourself is the situation, person or issue you are angry about or at, worth shortening your life? I wish I could tell you a resounding NO or a HELL NO, but it is up to you to determine your response and not allow anger to rob you of joy or precious time, that you will never get back.

I wish I could tell you that expressing uncontrol anger is not worth it. My father once told me, "Never argue with a fool, because folks watching won't know who's the fool, i.e., you or the person you are debating." I wish I could tell you that stuff happens, it is your choice on how you allow it to affect you and how you react to stuff that 6 months later you won't either remember or it won't matter anyway.

How you express your anger, affects others. This is so important… what you say or do towards others have a lasting impact. Saying something in anger towards someone hurts. Think about when you have hurt yourself and you have a physical scare that reminds you of the incident when and how you got the scare. While you may be sorry and apologize for something you said or did, there still may be an emotional scar that takes a while for someone else to heal beyond your apology. Words and actions can't be taken back as if they never happened when you do or say something in anger.

I wish I could tell you to learn to be in control of your emotions and "acting out" is not a way to get your way! I wish I could tell you that words are very powerful and destructive. Be careful, very careful with what you say and how you say things, regardless of what emotional state you may be. Words can really hurt others. Be careful what words you say to yourself mentally as well. Be kind, gracious and caring, even when you need to make strong statements whether to others or yourself.

My dear, many people will cross your path. I wish I could tell you that some are meant to be a part of your life for many years and others, are only intended to be in your life for a short season. I wish I could tell you how to be discerning about which is which, and why, but you will learn by listening, observing, examining, and studying what they say and do, as well as what they don't say and don't do. I wish I could tell you that some will say and do things that are contrary to what they have said and done previously. Others will be consistent in what they do and what they say. I wish I could tell you to study both because inconsistency can be the same as that that is consistent. Is there is honesty, kindness, sincerity, empathy, compassion and concern beyond themselves or are they only concerned with their own agenda?

I wish I could tell you to develop the ability to let go

and not waste time with folks who are only about themselves and not genuine about their friendship/relationship with you. I wish I could tell you that in the long term, you will be better off. I so wish I could tell you to make sure that you are genuine, honest, and caring beyond YOURSELF!

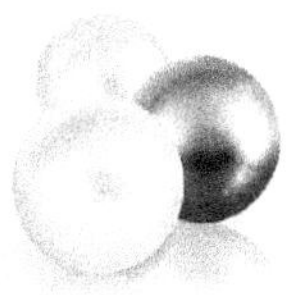

I wish I could tell you that you must know who you are and who you ain't, because there will always be folks that will try to define you, your abilities and what is possible for you. I gotta tell you that sometimes others want to feel comfortable with you based on their own comfort level. That is, if they have a need to be superior, they just might be critical, sarcastic, or demeaning to put you down.

Do not allow people who are insecure, jealous, or petty to undermine your self-confidence and self-worth. Always be open for constructive criticism and genuine feedback intended to help you, BUT be aware of the person's true intentions. I wish I could tell you to remember we are all a part of the construction crew. Some crew members tear down, and others build up. What role is the person offering you input or friendly advice operating? Examine the role you are playing and why, i, e. are you tearing down or building up? Be very conscious and conscientious of what you are tearing down, never hesitating to roll up your sleeves to build up as conscientiously as tearing down. Be fair and kind.

Pearl #14:
I wish I could tell you
that there will be situations.

I wish I could tell you that you will have situations and discussions that the person or individuals you are having the discussion might fall in the following categories. There are people that you will not need to give an explanation because for them it is not necessary. There are other people that an explanation is not possible, for a variety of reason, most significantly, some people simply do not want to understand, they might just want to argue, prove you wrong/prove themselves right, try to make you look/feel foolish and a variety of self-fulfilling reasons. I wish I could tell you that when folk are trippin', just let them take the trip **ALL** by themselves. I wish I could tell you to think about making a choice to not buy a ticket on someone else's trip. Please let them trip without taking you along physically or mentally or spiritually. I wish I could tell you that there are folks who just are a trip!

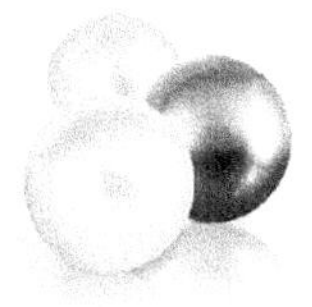

Pearl #15:
I wish I could tell you
how important your health is.

I wish I could tell you that to have balance in your life is extremely important to your overall well-being. First of all, your health has a lot to do with the choices you make about what you eat or don't eat, what you do or don't do with your body, what you put or don't put in your body, how much rest you get, and having a balance between working hard, studying hard and being able to have fun. Learn to relax. Allow yourself to laugh at yourself sometimes. Be silly. Make the choice to be happy with whatever life brings your way, by "dealing" with the ups and downs, as well as taking care of your physical, mental, and spiritual health!

I wish I could tell you that the length of your life is fueled by how you take care of yourself, but more important than the length, is the quality of your life and how you choose to live it. I wish I could tell you that you leave a part of you everywhere you go, with every person you meet and in everything you do. I wish I could tell you to leave every place, person, and activity better than they would have been, because of you.

Pearl #16:
I wish I could tell you
that you will be faced with hard choices.

I wish I could tell you that you may sometimes be faced with hard choices dealing with the choices that your friends make. I wish I could tell you that just because a friend is making an unwise choice, I hope you will make the best choice for you, even when a friend may put pressure on you or even make fun of you. It may be so difficult to choose differently than your friends. You may even feel all alone but make the wise choice to not get into trouble, to not do something dumb and especially to not do something that can affect your short- and long-term well-being. It is okay to be different, to not fit in.

Often, a person who has aspirations find themselves being alone. It is hard for others to understand you or your dreams. Remember, it is okay to be different, because God made you unique for the plans He has for you. Real friends and people who really care about you, will not entice you to do stupid things. Keep in mind that some people want you to go along with what they are doing or saying or thinking. PJ, don't be a "go along" to "get along" person. Often to go along, means you have to give up who you are, your values, and your sense of self-worth.

I wish I could tell you to not be afraid to say YES to what you want and to what you want to do, but to also be brave enough to say NO to what you don't want, as well as to what/who may not be in your best interest! My dear, don't buy a ticket on a trip you that the cost is too much to pay. Don't take a trip you don't want to take, nor is not in your best interest! Picture a plane taking off and think, "bye bye, take your solo flight, without me, PJ." Be proud that you have the good sense to say, no thank you. Go, but without PJ!

Pearl #17:
I wish I could tell you about the story you tell yourself.

I wish I could tell you that no two people see, think, or feel the same about a shared event. Let's say you have a disagreement with someone, and you feel one way about what the other person did or said, and if you talk to the other person, they might say that is not what they meant, or you took it the wrong way. So, what story do you tell yourself? In your mind, do you say to yourself, I know I am right about what happened, even though the other person sees it differently. OR, let's say you had an expectation from someone, and they didn't fill your expectation. Do you tell yourself an explanation of the other persons intention that is negative, even though you really don't know what happened or why?

What if the other person didn't even know about your expectation? I wish I could tell you that sometimes we tell ourselves stories that may not be true or stories that are a result of our own insecurities or our need to be right. There are some people who see themselves as victims, when things don't go their way or when others don't meet their expectations. I wish I could tell you to be honest in examining the stories that you tell yourself. Make sure you have the facts, and above all don't act based on what you perceive.

Ask yourself why are you thinking this way? Do you have enough information to form an opinion? Are you hurt? If so, why are you hurt? Learn to go to the other person and get more information about what or why and get clarification. Share your perception and ask if your perception is in alignment with what their perception of what happened.

So many people get angry with others, and even say or do things in anger based on the stories they tell themselves without getting clarification. Just because you think it, does not make it accurate or true. Would you want someone to treat you with anger or resentment or rejection without them telling you their perception of an incident that is the source of their response towards you? That simply is unfair, and unproductive. Sometimes relationships are lost or damaged unnecessarily and irreparably when a constructive, clarity information seeking conversation for understanding would have made the difference!

I wish I could tell you to swallow your pride and muster the courage to talk with the other person before you lose someone that you care about over something that just might be a misunderstanding. It is important to better understand what happened and why. I wish I could tell you to be the bigger person and to get the facts before you react.

Pearl #18:
I wish I could tell you that life will always be easy and wonderful.

It would be nice if I could tell you that these pearls would guarantee a perfect, happy, successful life. It just wouldn't be true. But I do believe that these pearls will help you navigate some of the troubled waters and winds of adversity you encounter. I really hope they do, but the lessons you must learn are unique and necessary specifically for you to be the person that God intend for you to be to fill the plan He has for you.

 So, the adversities in your life are so necessary for you to become the strong, courageous, and resilient person you were born to be. So, I wish I could tell you that in every situation, especial those that are adverse or challenging, ask yourself, what is the lesson for me to learn and what characteristic am I developing in this situation? Is this an opportunity for me to show compassion or forgiveness.

 Am I learning to be unselfish in sharing what I have?

Am I learning to not judge others? Do I need to not jump to conclusions about the motives, shortcomings, or intentions of others? Do I know how to love unconditionally with prudence, meaning sometimes we have to love others when they are not loveable. And then there are times when we have people who cross our paths, and their intentions are simply not good.

Sometimes we need to give some folk the gift of our absence. Be wise about who you give your time, your space, and especially your heart. Are they worthy? Are you worthy? I wish I could tell you, but PJ, you have to know and learn for yourself!

As strange as it may be, we tend to learn best who we are and who we ain't in adverse situations and with toxic people. I've come to learn that adversity gets us out of auto pilot mode. Adversity requires us to be more aware of what is going on. Adversity requires you, PJ, to examine more closely your own behavior, the behavior of others and the situations you find yourself.

Each element becomes more prevalent in understanding if you behaved yourself in to it? Did your choices create it or if others are creating it? Or, if life brought it to you to provide an opportunity for you to demonstrate your problem solving skills? Or your ability to be resilient "in spite" of the circumstance, such as illness or other unplanned, unexpected or unwanted events or people. Or how to deal with "toxic" people or individuals who simply "show up" differently than you. Or your ability to stretch yourself out of your comfort zone to meet someone in a way that creates a solution that works for both of you.

I wish I could tell you that in doing so you are demonstrating versatility and adaptation. You gain, rather than loose. You are the winner in these adverse situations, and in spite of someone who may be toxic or simply operating differently than you. I wish I could tell you to keep in mind that "different" is just that different, not necessarily wrong or bad, just different! What is "right" for you, may be "wrong" for someone else and vice versa.

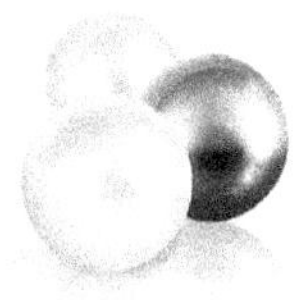

Pearl #19:
I wish I could be around to see...

I wish I could be around to see you live your life and deal with all that your life will entail. I have lived my life. I have learned many lessons. Whatever regrets I have, I have either given forgiveness to others, but mostly forgiven myself. I am human and not perfect, but I hope others will know I never intended to hurt, even though I might have.

As I consider some things while looking back, I would do differently because I learned a better way. Life is about learning and growing, always learning, especially about yourself. What makes you tick? What are your areas of vulnerability and insecurity? We all have them, but to grow beyond them is one of the keys to living a great life. What is important is to be able to look in the mirror at yourself and know, "When I knew better, I did better!"

I believe that we all will have an accountability to God about how we lived our lives and what we did with what He gave us, such as our talents and skills; our blessings and favor; our answered prayers; and the people who crossed our paths to teach us what we needed to know. How did you show up? What did you do to make a situation or another individual better?

I wish I could tell you, to acknowledge and give thanks to God for all he has done/given, is doing/giving and will do/give. NO ONE makes it totally on their own. It is like you can have a fancy car, but there are many factors that make that fancy car go. Some we understand and some we don't. Some we can explain and some we can't. Some we can fix and some we can't. But we are thankful when we put the key in the ignition the vehicle goes and runs as we need it to. Just as in life, there are parts we get and understand, as well as others, we know exist, we may not understand what and why, we just know in our hearts, mind and soul that they are essential to our existence.

My PJ, you are my Pure Joy and my Precious Jewel. I am so thankful for the time we have had. I prayed for you before you were conceived and was born. I prayed for all of our family and asked God, Our Father, the Almighty to bless, shower with His Grace, Favor, Provision and Protection for all generations to come. I wish I could tell you that I know He loves you, but you have to SEEK Him for yourself and WANT a relationship with Him. He wants a relationship with you. God wants you to want Him in your life. Believe me, life is better believing in God, than believing you don't need Him. I have found a sense of peace, joy, security happiness, purpose, direction, comfort and so much more that I don't have words to describe believing and living my life with having God as a central part of it!

There are blessings, unbelievable blessings in your life. I pray that you will have discernment and an open mind to recognize the blessings, grace, favor, and touch from God when they happen with gratitude and humility. I am so very thankful for you, my precious jewel of pure joy! I love you!

I pass these pearls of Grannie's wisdom, lessons learned, and lessons earned to you. Yep… I wish you will read and learn for yourself! Enjoy the journey, even the bumpy parts. Wonderful adventures await!

PJ, you have the DNA of some strong women in you. Miss Nellie (Palmer), your great-great grandmother, Miss Helen (Walker), my mom and your Great grandmother, Miss Tena, your mom and me, Grannie! We all have had our share and often more than our share of adversity and lessons we learned. So, whatever lies ahead and whatever you have already experienced remember you are strong, able and are victorious when it is all said and done. Make the best decision that you can, and make better decision when you know better. You go girl, Grannie's PJ and God's precious gift!

Grannie loves you, my PJ, with all of my heart.
Thank you for being my PJ!

I wish I could know that you know how thankful
I am to have had you as my special PJ!

And how much pure joy you gave me!

Luv ya,
Grannie

"Quotes from James A. Michener"

"The master in the art of living makes little distinction between his work and his play, his labor and his leisure, his mind and his body, his information and his recreation, his love, and his religion. He hardly knows which is which. He simply pursues his vision of excellence at whatever he does, leaving others to decide whether he is working or playing. To him he always doing both."

"If a man happens to find himself, he has a mansion which he can inhabit with dignity all the days of his life."

"For this is the journey that men and women make, to find themselves. If they fail in this, it doesn't matter much else what they find."

A summary of Grannie's rambling

-Savor every day's lessons, whether joyful or challenging, the lessons are building blocks

-Don't wait for change, be the change, create the change, encourage the change

-Don't excuse someone else's unwillingness to change or allow it to affect you embracing the progress that change will bring to your journey.

-Perfect how you do your process of change, so it will be efficient, invited, and painless

-Don't try to lay a foundation of permanency, where you should only pitch a tent. Some situations, things and people only have a temporary place in your life and others are lifelong – know the difference.

-Discover your passion in what you would do for free, or you would be willing to pay someone to let you do!

-It is your life based on the choices you make. Learn from the consequences or benefits of the choices you make.

-Map your own journey; don't buy a ticket on someone else's trip. Let them take a solo flight.

-Words are very powerful, once spoken cannot be erased. Never say anything, that you will regret and will damage significant relationships. Saying I'm sorry, never erases the damage a thoughtless comment makes, even though the act is forgiven.

-There will be times when you will be afraid to do something you need to do. Do it anyway! Don't let your fears of failure hold you back. Failure only exists when you don't step out even when afraid. What people will or won't say is of no consequence. It is what you say to yourself in your thoughts and actions that truly matters.

-The level of trust can be responsible for the success or failure of any relationship or endeavor

-Be trustworthy

Grannie's Questions for you PJ

My PJ what did you read that at this time is most significant? Please put date.

PJ what was most difficult for you to read and understand.

PJ, at this particular time, what/who are you struggling with? Describe situation and/or individual.

PJ, at this particular time, what ideas or actions can/should you work on? What is your timeline for addressing? What is the outcome you want?

PJ, at this particular time, what are you Most proud of? Describe

PJ, what's next?

PJ, what is most important to you at this time?

PJ, what is least important to you at this time?

PJ, who are you and what are your aspirations?

PJ, pray and ask the Holy Spirit for guidance, direction and peace for your aspirations and what you want to do.

"NOTES – THOUGHTS"